WATCH YOUR STEP!

Contents

**Diana Bentley
and Sylvia Karavis**

**Story illustrated by
Andrés Martinez**

Heinemann

In this story

 Cool Cat

 The children

Tricky words

- children
- bridge
- hurray
- stay
- across
- waved
- whoops

Introduce these tricky words and help the reader when they come across them later!

Story starter

When Cat hears a cry for help he turns into Cool Cat. One day, Cat was sleeping near a rope bridge when he heard some children shouting for help.

Cool Cat and the Rope Bridge

"Help!" said the children.
"Look at the bridge."

"This is a job for Cool Cat," said Cat.
"I will help the children."

"Hurray for Cool Cat!"
said the children.
"Cool Cat will help us!"

"Stay cool," said Cool Cat.
"I can help you."

"Cool Cat is cool,"
said the children.
"Now we can get across."

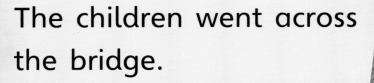

The children went across
the bridge.

"Thank you, Cool Cat," said the children.

"Cool," said Cool Cat.

The children waved to Cool Cat.

Cool Cat waved to
the children.

"Look out, Cool Cat!"
said the children.

"Whoops!" said Cool Cat.

Quiz

Text Detective

- How did Cool Cat help the children?
- What did Cool Cat do wrong?

Word Detective

- **Phonic Focus:** Initial letter sounds
  Page 4: Find a word beginning with the phoneme 'j'.
- Page 4: Find three words starting with a capital letter.
- Page 6: Find a word that rhymes with 'play'.

Super Speller

Read these words:

look   for   now

Now try to spell them!

HA! HA! HA!

Q What is the shortest bridge in the world?

A The bridge of your nose!

13

Find out about

- Some bridges that fell down

Tricky words

- most
- bridges
- strong
- people
- boat
- over
- road

Introduce these tricky words and help the reader when they come across them later!

Text starter

Most bridges are built across water. Some bridges are built for trains and cars to go across. Some bridges are for people to walk across. Most bridges are very strong but sometimes bridges fall down.

Bridge Disasters

Most bridges are very strong.

This bridge is very strong.

People said this bridge was very strong but it was not.

One day a boat hit the bridge and it fell down.

Four cars went into the river.

This bridge went over a road.

People said the bridge was very strong.

Then one day it fell down on to the road.

People said this bridge was very strong but it was not.

Strong winds caused this bridge to collapse.

One day it fell down.

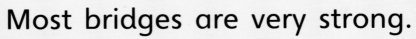

Most bridges are very strong.

Most bridges do not fall down.

Quiz

Text Detective

- Why do bridges need to be strong?
- Have you ever travelled over a bridge?

Word Detective

- **Phonic Focus:** Initial letter sounds
  Page 15: Find a word beginning with the phoneme 'v'.
- Page 15: Find a word that rhymes with 'wrong'.
- Page 17: Find a word meaning 'bumped into'.

Super Speller

Read these words:

are day fall

Now try to spell them!

HA! HA! HA!

Q Why didn't the skeleton cross the bridge?

A He didn't have the guts!